SMARTER
CLEANER
LEANER

Feed Your Brain,
Not Your Stomach

ALKAWTHER
MAKKI

STRATTON
—PRESS—

Publishing Life

Stratton Press Publishing
831 N Tatnall Street Suite M #188,
Wilmington, DE 19801
www.stratton-press.com
1-888-323-7009

ISBN (Paperback): 978-1-64345-948-6
ISBN (Ebook): 978-1-64345-949-3

Printed in the United States of America

LIFESTYLE CATALOG

ABSTRACT

An optimum healthy lifestyle that interacts with all body systems, is taught by a system of nutrient health principles, whole food elements, and implements health practices that preserve health, seeks prevention, and improves quality of life and self-efficacy as well as increasing stamina, agility, and vitality.

Why do you eat what you eat for breakfast?

You were taught to eat cereal with milk, cream cheese, bagels, waffles, pancakes, sausage, toast, and jam, which will set you up for failure when choosing the right foods for your second meal.

Solution: How about eating vegetables and fruits for breakfast, or a more traditional avocado and eggs for a healthy start.

Is breakfast really the most important meal of the day?

No, it is not, not by a long shot. What is important is what you eat when you do breakfast.

Solution: eating as soon as you wake up is not as healthy as you were taught to believe. Your body actually gains fuel and energy when you intermittently fast. When you eat breakfast around noon, 1:00 or 2:00 p.m., you should choose your food wisely so that your second meal around five to seven hours later will be chosen confidently.

SMARTER
Cleaner
Leaner

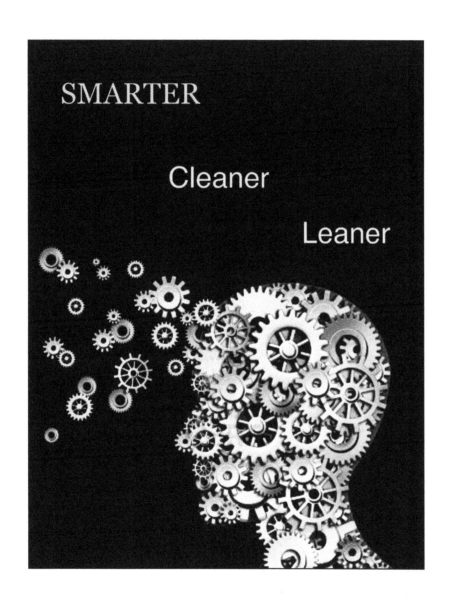

INTRODUCTION

Today you are reading this because you are making an effort to change your life, in whatever part, form, or magnitude. Are you fed up with promising health plans and seeking an honest long term solution, or you are motivated and inspired to make a change? Have you struggled with weight loss, or have you been lethargic, weak, and continue to battle health ailments? Whatever your motives, you are here because you want to feel different and ultimately become your best self.

It took you six months to crawl, one year to walk, and two years to run. How many years will it take you to take control of your life and feel that you are who you were born to be—strong, intelligent, talented, and resilient? How many times have you said that you will start tomorrow, next week, after Thanksgiving, after the holidays, after your birthday, or after that upcoming party? The truth is you continue to make excuses because plans have failed you before, and you only found temporary solutions where hard efforts never paid off. Do not be hard on yourself; you were taught misleading eating habits, practices, and proposed solutions. Have you considered making a lifelong change? Does *lifelong* sound too farfetched and impossible because you still want to enjoy your favorite pizza or chocolate cake with vanilla bean ice cream? I am not saying you can no longer enjoy your pizza or cake; rather, learn to savor real human food and attain human practices because you are valuable and worthy of owning your best self.

Today is your tomorrow and tomorrow starts today. Today you will start the age of discovery by relearning and establishing what human food is. One might ask how an advanced society is subject to relearn what we were once naturally born with and practiced for thousands of years. It is clear that our ethics and principles have been altered by competitive markets and greedy profits. It is already difficult to meet ends meet, especially if you are raising a family that requires healthy food and proper clothing. Foods labeled as organic are more expensive than those that are not, but why do they have to be? Many Americans do not have the financial means to consume organic foods on a daily basis, thus making right health choices intimidating. Then there are those who grow up in bad environments, who lack the knowledge and proper nutrition because they are constant subjects of abuse, drugs, and improper sanitation. It is degrading that our health has become a business opportunity that has focused less on human nutrition and more on weight loss. More than ever, doctors are rethinking what they once believed about saturated fats, the causes of diabetes and cholesterol. It seemed for the longest time we encountered an era like the dark ages, and now we are Michelangelos, relearning the skills and techniques that our ancestors already used thousands of years ago. Today you will rise like the age of the Enlightenment after the Dark Ages.

On the positive side, as a nation, we have become more health conscious by making tremendous efforts to encourage exercise and healthier eating habits. People have been seeking healthier food choices, and accordingly, grocery markets have engaged in the organic niche and there is an increased hype for exercise outlets in the business sector. On the downside, there is a negative impact to the modern health trend. Companies and markets are competitively creating products and advertising them to be the miracle in weight loss; such even suggest that they can achieve this weight loss without altering their selection of food or without exercise. The pills make you lose weight by blocking fat absorption, and while this may be true, what is the negative impact on your health? People are often led into the wrong direction because what they are offered is promising; however, they are unaware that there is an opportunity cost (focusing and seeking one plan or action and losing efficiency in another). While the end result is physically satisfying, one can become blindsided by the detrimental side effects. Our brain relies on healthy foods that contain fats, carbs, and proteins for function and mental performance. Fats are found in organic foods such as eggs, avocados, walnuts, and coconuts. Ask yourself, if you are taking a pill that blocks the absorption of fats, does it also block the absorption of healthy fats and nutrients that is essential to your brain health? Make sure that while you are shrinking your waist size, you are not shrinking your organs in the process. To a greater extreme, there are a plethora of health articles suggesting that brain health is heavily reliant on saturated fats. This is a bizarre overgeneralization. If your food consist mostly of red meats that are high in saturated fats, you are setting yourself up for numerous health illnesses. There are foods high in carbohydrates and proteins that contribute to your brain health because the food contains essential vitamins, nutrients, and amino acids. Foods have their own genetic makeup; therefore, it is wrong to conclude that saturated fats alone are optimum for your brain health.

Key factors to keep in mind before beginning your lifestyle guide. What you eat and consume is primary; however, exercise is secondary, just like research. If you are faced with a question or are interested in a product, often you seek secondary research from online sites, articles, or reviews. Be confident that what you will learn today is mostly primary research, experience and experiment based on trial and error. When we have a question of how things work, we need to identify the test subjects, conduct the research, and test the hypothesis. Many people just want to lose weight and look great; however, does that really get to the root cause of an underlying problem? Does it make you feel healthier if your weight loss is in part successful due to limited calories and starvation? I do *not* believe that you can eat whatever you want and still be at your best, as long as you regulate calories and exercise. While you might lose weight, you will also lose strength and vitality. I could lose a substantial amount of weight just by consuming bread and doughnuts. In retrospect, what do those foods do to my liver, kidneys, eyes, brain, and organs? Your brain will not be as sharp and your heart may be subject to clogged arteries due to sugar uptake and trans fats.

Finally, who wants to count calories for the rest of their life? I believe counting calories is no way to live and it certainly is an act you may engage in for some period of time and later disregard completely. I do not count calories and you shouldn't either. You might ask, then how do we lose weight? Did our ancestors count calories before? No, they consumed the right food at the right time. They certainly did not engage in eating six times a day, or even three times a day. They did not continuously snack anytime they had a craving, and did they feel all the crazy spontaneous cravings we feel now? No, they rarely, if ever, consumed sugar and hybridized wheat, both of which cause cravings. They ate einkorn wheat, which if consumed by people with gluten sensitivities today would not cause them to have stomach issues, allergies, or reactions. Six hundred fifty calories of cake is not equal to 650 calories of a fatty fish with vegetables. When you eat a cake, you are feeding your stomach. On the other hand, when you eat a fatty fish with vegetables, you will feel full and satiated, more importantly you are feeding your brain. There are plenty of sources that are higher in calories if consumed that will help aid in weight loss, opposed to if you ate a low-calorie food empty on essential nutrients. So forget those calories; they are misleading as well as intimidating…just act like they don't exist.

Let's identify a problem, introduce the causes and effects, and seek a potential solution.

Problem: Our nation is one of the most obese with rising illnesses despite its efforts to be more health conscious.

Causes: Our nation consumes sugar, red meat, and artificial ingredients at an alarming rate. All the while we make conscious efforts to consume healthier food choices, unfortunately, we are subject to toxic pesticides and glyphosate that make their way into our farmlands. Our atmosphere has become polluted due to increased industrialization and technological advancements.

Effects: Our health as individuals as well as a nation is suffering with an increased rate of cancer, diseases, and mental illnesses. Pollution alone impacts are health in tremendous ways. In addition, imagine the overload of toxins and chemicals from the foods we consume on our bodies and organs. We are constantly bombarded with free radicals that shorten and damage our cells.

Solution: Be mindful by choosing foods that are traceable and have been tested and certified for purity. Be in support of humane practices by imposing cleaner ways of living to reduce CO_2 in the environment. Make an effort to reduce the consumption of sugar and sugar in other forms, which pose numerous health risks. In addition, sugar is a poison that needs to be eradicated or regulated. Legally, sugar may be regulated in various ways. First, by implementing laws that reduces the amount of sugar per serving, raising the price of sugar while lowering the cost of the healthier natural alternative so that the average consumer will consume less or make use of the inferior good. Red meat is not human food. Our bodies and brains are not meant or equipped to break down animal proteins, thus we do not have the same enzymes and canines as carnivores. Eat cleaner by consuming less red meat and opt for plant foods.

If you are in your late teens or early twenties, eating all the food you crave and continue to feel great, think again. You are not the exception. Eventually the sugar accumulates in your body, the chemicals and toxins disrupt your organ functions, and unhealthy habits will wreak havoc on your life, suddenly and unexpectedly. Make right choices now, for yourself and for the environment. Moreover, the health of the environment will determine the purity and potency of your food. It is frantic and dehumanizing that the wild caught fish on our dinner plates just might be loaded with toxins, plastics, and pharmaceutical drugs due to human biocides entering oceans.

IDENTIFYING FALSE CLAIMS

False claim:	At age 6, I remember doctors advocating the consumption of tap water for healthier teeth and organs because it contains fluoride.
The truth:	Fluoride is a poison. The fluoride that is added to our drinking water is not the same fluoride that naturally exists in our bodies.
False claim:	As a child, I remember my parents would cook with margarine instead of butter and purchase fat-free milk because doctors claimed that saturated fats were the cause of weight gain and heart problems.
The truth:	Butter is healthier than margarine. Saturated fats from natural foods aid in weight loss.
False claim:	At age 12, I remember health gurus and doctors telling people that eating six times a day was a healthy way of eating right and that would help them lose more weight.
The truth:	Eating six times a day is not healthy. Continued food consumption promotes high insulin levels and works your organs in overtime.
False claim:	In my teens, there was all the hype with sugar-free snacks that were healthier options for diabetics.
The truth:	Those sugar-free snacks and sodas are replaced with artificial sweeteners that actually make you gain more weight and disrupt your brain neurons.

False claim:	I am sure you are familiar with those fat-free chips with the magic ingredient Olean, advertising the word *lean* in efforts to make you believe it would make you leaner.
The truth:	Olean does not make you lose weight; in fact, it blocks your body from absorbing nutrients and creates stomach problems.
False claim:	Ten years ago, people were seeking milk alternatives, mainly due to their lactose intolerances and reduced fat content. Soy milk and almond milk became the two familiar alternatives that people still prefer today.
The truth:	Soy milk and almond milk most likely contain carrageenan or gums; they are thickeners or stabilizers, which are artificially produced. The gums disrupt your digestive tract and could cause an array of stomach problems, including inflammation.
False claim:	Five years ago, the gluten-free motto still reigns in. Gluten free is healthier than wheat.
The truth:	While gluten free is healthier than hybridized wheat, it is not healthy as perceived to be because there are ingredients that are not any cleaner or healthier. Most gluten-free products contain ingredients such as rice flour that contains high level of arsenic, hydrolyzed vegetable protein, and sugar, all of which make you gain weight.
False claim:	Doctors claiming that coconut oil and eggs contribute to bad cholesterol and are not heart friendly; therefore it is better not to consume them.
The truth:	Coconut oil and eggs are super healthy for your brain and your overall health. Sugar causes bad cholesterol, heart diseases, and clogged arteries.
False claim:	Breakfast (eating early morning) is the most important meal of the day.
The truth:	You should not eat as soon as you get up; what you eat when you do break-fast is important.

Ever think about other factors that affect your physical and mental health beyond food and exercise? It is vital that we address other factors and take them into consideration because we practice them daily and they affect how we feel and how we think in momentous ways.

Several questions to ask yourself and take a few moments to think about:

What do I wash my face, hands, and body with?
What products do I shower my hair with?
What type of water do I consume?
What utensils do I cook my food with?
What clothing fabrics am I wearing?
What detergents do I wash my clothes with?
What chemicals are in my colognes and perfumes?
What is in my deodorant?
What habits do I have?

Now that we have given you an overview and some background information, we can get started with your essential guide.

WHO AM I ?

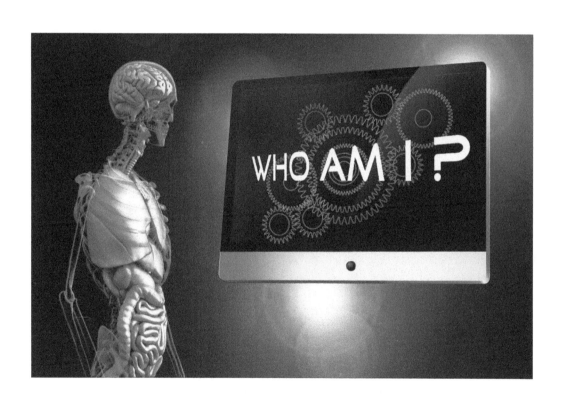

FAT LOSS STRATEGIC PLAN

Contractual—commit to the strategy

- drink one table spoon of organic apple cider vinegar with 8 ounces glass of water, morning or before bedtime
- two meals per day
- at least five hours and not more than seven hours between your first and second meal
- one glass of room temperature water upon waking up or one glass of celery root juice
- do not drink artificially alkalized water
- one quart of room temperature water / complete drinking one hour before each meal
- last meal at least three hours before bedtime
- intermittent fasting of thirteen to eighteen hours between supper (dinner) and breakfast (your first meal) the next morning
- It is not required to exercise during the first thirty days of this strategy.
- You should exercise before your first meal of the day. However, you should exercise as your schedule permits.
- You may still drink your coffee or tea, however, *without* sugar or creamer.

Staple—important and required

- water that is fluoride free, chromium free, BPA and BPS free
- wild-caught seafood
- Redmond's Real Salt, Himalayan salt, or Celtic Sea Salt
- organic avocado oil for cooking meals and organic olive oil for dressings
- organic unsalted butter
- organic eggs
- only naturally occurring sugars in fruits and vegetables allowed

Overgenerous—These food are allowed; however, consume them at minimum.

- organic gluten-free oatmeal
- organic peanut butter that is no added salt and no added sugar
- organic whole grass milk
- organic grass-fed cheese
- organic einkorn wheat / ancient wheat

Collation—Incorporate these foods in place of desert or snacking, allowed one per each meal. Do not wait more than ten minutes to consume after your meals, or your insulin levels will rise and it will be considered snacking.

Fruits (organic)—choose one

- apple
- kiwi
- banana (greener in color)
- blueberries
- strawberries
- blackberries
- raspberries
- grapes
- watermelon
- cantaloupe
- apricot
- mulberries
- goji berries
- golden berries
- acai berries
- elderberry
- plum
- prunes
- dragon fruit
- pomegranate
- mangosteen

Seeds—choose one

- hemp seed
- chia seed
- flaxseed
- sunflower seed
- pumpkin seed

Nuts (organic)—choose one

- walnuts/handful
- pecans/handful
- almonds/handful
- Brazil nuts / three nuts maximum

Teas—are a great way to build your immunity as well as enhance your cognition. If you feel the urge to snack after your meal, think about having a cup of tea, preferably caffeine-free herbal tea. Teas are a great way to ease your cravings and get you through the night.

- green tea
- black tea
- oolong tea
- chamomile tea
- peppermint tea
- ginger tea
- hibiscus tea
- Echinacea tea
- rooibos tea
- sage tea
- rosehip tea
- passion flower tea
- lemon balm tea
- turmeric tea
- licorice tea

Contraband—prohibited and impermissible

- GMO (genetically modified organism)
- sugar, fructose, cane sugar, brown sugar, high-fructose corn syrup, corn syrup, corn syrup solids, agave nectar, brown rice syrup, glucose, dextrose, dextrin, diastatic malt, ethyl maltol, barley malt, rice syrup
- foods high in lectins: cashews, tomato, soybeans, potato, beans, lentils, legumes, eggplant
- milk and milk alternatives that contain sugar, carrageenan, or gums
- artificial sweeteners
- snacking
- tap water / fluoride water
- red meat
- farm-raised seafood
- fried food
- canned food
- prepackaged food
- protein bars and shakes
- orange juice and other juices
- sodas, energy drinks, carbonated drinks
- sauces / store-bought condiments
- dressings / premixed seasonings
- hybridized wheats / refined grains / bread
- iodized salt
- creamer
- cereal
- rice
- corn

MACRONUTRIENTS

Macronutrients are sources of nutrients needed for energy and body functions.

Focusing on macros is far more important than calorie counting.

The following food need to be organic; these are examples of foods that you should incorporate into your meals but not limited to the following:

Proteins—chicken, fish, eggs, avocado, teff, hempseed, spirulina, amaranth, quinoa, chia seeds, pumpkin seeds, broccoli, spinach, asparagus, artichokes, Brussels sprouts, green peas(in small amounts)

Fats—avocados, unsweetened dark chocolate, whole eggs, wild-caught sardines, wild-caught fatty fish, walnuts, almonds, Brazil nuts, pecans, pistachios, cottage cheese, extra virgin olive oil, unsalted butter, almond butter, chia seeds, flax seeds, coconut, coconut oil, and olives

Carbohydrates—oatmeal, quinoa, sweet potatoes, apples, blueberries, beets, pumpkin, butternut squash, zucchini, green beans, carrots, cucumbers, spinach, broccoli, kale, onions, and dandelion root

MICRONUTRIENTS

Micronutrients are essential elements to maintain your health.

Focusing on micronutrients is more important than taking vitamin supplements.

The following nutrients and amino acids should be incorporated in your meals:

Essential Amino Acids—important to your body functions

- *Glutathione* is vital in protecting your cells against oxidative damage and is found in spinach, broccoli, almonds, walnuts, and grass-fed whey protein.
- *Histidine* is vital in immune responses and sleep-wake cycles, and is found in fish.
- *Isoleucine* is vital in muscle tissue and hemoglobin and are found in cottage cheese.
- *Lysine* is vital in collagen production and is found in fish, eggs, and quinoa.
- *Phenylalanine* is vital in endorphin production and preventing mood swings and is found in fish.
- *Threonine* is vital in formation of cartilage, skin, hair, nails, and function of small intestines and are found in cottage cheese.
- *Valine* is vital in muscle growth and energy production and is found in fish, eggs, cottage cheese, chicken, and nuts.
- *Tryptophan* is vital in serotonin production, boosts mood, regulates sleep and appetite, and is found in chicken breasts, chia seeds, pumpkin, halibut, and salmon.

- *Leucine* is vital in regulating blood sugar levels, wound healing, and fatigue and is found in beets.
- *Methionine* is vital in growth and development and is found in Brazil nuts, Parmesan cheese, chicken breast, and fish.

Vitamins—essential nutrients that boost the immune system and cell repair. Your vitamin sources need to be obtained through consuming organic whole foods and not vitamin supplements.

- *Vitamin A / Retinoid*—obtained from carrots, pumpkin, sweet potatoes
- *Vitamin B1 / Thiamine*—obtained from watermelon, pine nuts, coriander
- *Vitamin B2 / Riboflavin*—obtained from almonds
- *Vitamin B3 / Niacin*—obtained from avocado
- *Vitamin B5 / Pantothenic Acid*—obtained from fish, avocado, eggs, lean chicken
- *Vitamin B6 / Pyridoxine*—obtained from ricotta cheese, salmon, eggs
- *Vitamin B7 / Biotin*—obtained from egg yolks, walnuts, pecans
- *Vitamin B9 / Folate*—obtained from spinach, asparagus, avocado, artichoke
- *Vitamin B12 / Cobalamin*—obtained from sardines, clams, tuna
- *Vitamin C / Ascorbic Acid*—obtained from Kakadu plum, camu, acerola cherries, thyme, parsley, kiwi, artichoke
- *Vitamin D / Cholecalciferol*—obtained from salmon, sardines, oysters, shrimp, egg yolks, shiitake mushrooms
- *Vitamin E / A-Tocopherol*—obtained from sunflower seeds, almonds, avocados, butternut squash, shrimp, asparagus
- *Vitamin K1 / Phylloquinone*—obtained from spinach, collards, Brussels sprouts, dandelion

Minerals—antioxidants to help you grow, develop, build strong organs and balance pH levels

Macro Minerals
- Calcium—found in poppy seeds, sesame seeds, chia seeds, Parmesan cheese
- Potassium—found in avocados, sweet potatoes, spinach
- Magnesium—found in dark chocolate, avocados, almonds
- Phosphorus—found in halibut, almonds, yellow fin tuna
- Sulfur—found in kale, cabbage, onions, garlic, broccoli
- Choline—found in eggs, cauliflower, shrimp
- Sodium—found in sea salt, beets

Trace Minerals
- Iodine—found in seaweed, seafood, kelp
- Selenium—found in Brazil nuts, yellow fin tuna, chicken, cottage cheese
- Iron—found in salmon, broccoli, spinach
- Manganese—found in mussels, sweet potatoes, pine nuts
- Copper—found in oysters, raw kale, prunes
- Zinc—found in Alaskan crab, pumpkin seeds, cocoa powder, kefir
- Cobalt—found in broccoli, spinach
- Chromium—found in shellfish, broccoli, Brazil nuts
- Molybdenum—found in peas, lentils, almonds, soy

Ionic Minerals
- Humic and Fulvic Acid (electrically charged nano-sized mineral)—antiviral and antibacterial, improves absorption of nutrients and removes toxic pollutants from your body. Should never be taken with chlorine, tap water, or fluoridated water.

Phytonutrients—antioxidants for immune health and prevention of cancer

Cartenoids—Found in Pumpkin and Carrots
- Lycopene—found in watermelon
- Lutein—found in spinach, kale
- Ellagic Acid—found in strawberries, raspberries, pomegranates

Flavonoids—found in plant foods
- Catechins—found in green tea
- Hesperidin—found in citrus
- Flavnols—found in apples, berries, onions

Resveratrol—found in grapes, purple grape juice
Glucosinolates—found in kale, broccoli, Brussels sprouts

Essential Nutrients—for brain and eye

- Omega 3—promotes brain health and mood
- CoQ10—reduces free radical damage
- Beta carotene—keeps lungs healthy and supports eye vision

FLAVOUR

Incorporate herbs and spices in your meals to increase immunity and metabolism.

Organic Spices

- *Cocoa*—full of flavonoids, boost heart health
- *Caraway Seeds*—reduces constipation, lowers cholesterol, prevents cancer
- *Black Pepper*—reduces inflammation, controls heart rate and blood pressure
- *Paprika*—promotes healthy circulation and increases serotonin
- *Garlic*—lowers risk of heart disease, stops growth of cancer cells
- *Cumin*—rich in iron, helps with weight loss
- *Turmeric*—anti-inflammatory, inhibits tumors
- *Ceylon Cinnamon*—anti-diabetic
- *Ginger*—treats nausea, anti-inflammatory
- *Cardamom*—sooths upset stomach, lowers blood pressure
- *Saffron*—relieves PMS and depression, fights infections and wounds
- *Cayenne Pepper*—fat burning, clears sinuses, regulates hormones
- *Cloves*—fights oral diseases, boosts immunity
- *Crushed Red Pepper*—boost metabolism, decreases hunger, sooths ulcers

Organic Herbs

- *Basil*—combats infections, cleans the liver, relieves joint pains
- *Oregano*—prevents chronic diseases, detoxifies, strengthens bones, and improves heart health, protects against diabetes
- *Rosemary*—enhances memory, fights bacteria, and prevents spoiling
- *Tarragon*—freshens breath, relieves tooth pain, expels parasitic worms
- *Thyme*—prevents pneumonia and diarrhea, reduces abdominal inflammation
- *Parsley*—inhibits breast cancer cell growth
- *Cilantro*—reduces rheumatic diseases, lowers cholesterol, stimulates digestion, helps regrow bones, removes heavy metals and toxins from your body, prevents smallpox
- *Peppermint*—reduces nausea, indigestion, improves brain function
- *Sage*—aids in brain function and memory, sooths sore throats
- *Fenugreek*—lowers blood sugar levels
- *Rosemary Extract*—natural preservative

FOOD STORAGE WASTE AND PREVENTION

Preparation

Think about what is really needed for the upcoming week to prevent rotting. I complete all my grocery shopping once per week.

When storing foods, familiarize expiration dates of perishable items. I like to store my walnuts, pecans, and almonds in the refrigerator because they can become rancid.

For raw foods like fruits and vegetables, store at the required temperature. I store apples, asparagus, carrots in the refrigerator. I store grapes, blueberries, and strawberries in a plastic bag with tiny holes for ventilation in the refrigerator. I wash my lettuce heads and wrap them in paper towels before storing. Melons, garlic, onions, and potatoes are stored at room temperature. I separate my onions far away from potatoes.

When cooking your food, consider serving amount for you and your family. I'm guilty of making too much food that sometimes gets thrown out after seconds.

Dine out less because you are not preparing your meals, therefore, you cannot track every ingredient. We are prone to waste when we dine out; we tend to order too much or overeat. I used to overeat every dine in…not anymore.☺

Helpful sites: 8fit.com, halfyourplate.ca, cleangreensimple.com, foodconstrude.com, helloglo.co, realsimple.com, stopwaste.org, thekitchn.com, wisebread.com

Chemicals—recognizing toxins and carcinogens in processed foods and removing them from your regimen because they are health hazards that can cause cancer

- *Fluoride*—mistaken for an essential part of human consumption; however, it is a poison added to drinking water and most toothpastes
- *Soy Lecithin*—a fatty substance that is used to smooth out food texture to get soy binding; hexane is used
- *Whey Protein*—a byproduct of dairy, low in micronutrients, is acidic, and produces mucus; found in protein shakes
- *Brown Rice Syrup*—sweetener that has a high glycemic index and high arsenic content; found in energy bars and sports drinks
- *High Fructose Corn Syrup*—an artificial sweetener made from cornstarch; increases triglyceride levels, far more addicting than sugar, easily converted into fat; found in many packaged foods, drinks, and condiments
- *Carrageenan*—used as a thickening agent in food products; causes cellular inflammation and increases insulin sensitivity; found in milkshakes and ice cream
- *Aspartame*—an artificial sweetener; can cause weight gain, seizures, headaches; found in sugar-free sodas, sugar-free ice cream, and sugarless candy
- *MSG*—a processed flavor enhancer; type of glutamates that messes with the chemicals in your brain; can cause headaches and heart irregularities; found in packaged and processed foods as well as restaurant foods to enhance flavor; labeled as other hidden names such as hydrolyzed protein
- *Olestra/Olean*—a synthetic oil and calorie-free food; made up of sugar and oil; mostly found in chips
- *Artificial Flavors/Color*—blue #1 and #2 , citrus red #2, green #3, red #3 and #40, yellow #5 and #6; causes headaches, allergies, hypersensitivity, genetic defects, ADHD; found in cereal, candy, juices
- *Preservatives (Sodium Benzoate, Potassium Benzoate, BHA, and Sodium Nitrate)*—added to prevent mold and spoilage; endocrine disruptors that causes thyroid damage; commonly found in lunchmeats
- *Herbicides and Pesticides* (Alachlor, Atrazine, Endothall)—chemicals are sprayed on our crops. Chemicals are endocrine disruptors that cause cancer. To avoid herbicide and pesticide, buy organic from your local farm. Soak fruits and vegetables in cold water for half an hour. For a quick wash, wash fruits and vegetables with an apple cider vinegar or salt.

MEAL KIT DELIVERIES

Although it is optimum and preferred to prepare meals yourself, I understand that sometimes the time and energy it takes to prepare a meal is not feasible, especially when you are juggling a career, school, household and family obligations. Grocery shopping, along with choosing all the right ingredients accustomed to your good intentions, sometimes doesn't play out as we may wish. Since 'Time' is of the essence and so is your health, I have compiled a list of organic meal deliveries services that provides meal kits tailored to your eating regimen to ensure you have the time and energy to consume healthy meals.

Are you a Vegan, Vegetarian, Keto or Paleo enthusiast?

Do you have Gluten, Dairy, Soy or Lectin sensitivities?

Is your nutriment based on low FODMAP foods?

Looking to try the Mediterranean or Raw food regime?

Would you like to enjoy a plethora of food sustenance while eating like a Real Human to feel Super Human?

When ordering your meal kits from the preferred delivery service of your choice, please be sure to read all ingredients and make sure that it follows the "Fat Loss Strategic Plan" along with (Contractual, Collation and Contraband) indicators. If I have listed suggested foods in the plan that you have sensitivities to, please only include the nutriment that is ideal to your health system and digestive tract. For Example: "apple" is an organic fruit I have suggested. If you are following a low FODMAP nutriment, an apple will not be your ideal choice of fruit; blueberries will make a better choice as well as choosing an unripe banana (green banana) opposed to a ripe banana. Neither is the food sustenance regimen limited to the fruits and vegetables list I have included in the indicators. I have merely provided suggestions that work well with the plan. In addition, it is important to **avoid** and **eliminate** those foods that I have specifically suggested, such as tomatoes and corn.

Home Chef	Green Chef	Sun Basket	Epicured
Hello Chef	Healthy Chef Creations	Bistro MD	Sakara Life
Fresh Direct	Every Plate	Dinnerly	Snap Kitchen
Freshly	Purple Carrot	Daily Harvest	Trifecta Nutrition
Fresh N Lean	Blue Apron	Terras Kitchen	Veestro
Fresh and Easy	Gobble	One Potato	Caveman Chefs
Freshology	Martha & Marley Spoon	Yumble	Urban Remedy
Factor 75	Paleo Power Meals	Underground prep	Ice Age Meals
Meal Pro	Hungry Root	Eatology	Kettle Bell Kitchen
Keto Fridge	Pete's Paleo	Ketoned Bodies	Paleo on the Go

HOLISTIC HEALING MODALITIES

Herbal medicines and essential oils are effective remedies to treat and heal one's body, mind, and soul. As I have used these remedies and practices to heal myself, they may not be the solution to heal you; therefore if you chose to use them, you are using them at your own will. I am not liable to any side effects encountered from the participant. What works for me will not always work for someone else; these are merely suggestions. If you decide to consume these, refer to the suggested use and servings for the appropriate amount to consume. Any of the mentioned herbs or oils may trigger allergic reactions; therefore speak with your healthcare provider before taking any of these. As with any medicine, interactions may occur.

Herbal Medicine

- *Bacopa moneri*—an adaptogen and diuretic. A nootropic herb that repairs damaged neurons and improves brain function, enhances memory, creativity, and cognitive drive.
- *Astragalus*—an herb from the root of a perennial plant. Astragals has been used in traditional Chinese medicine for centuries. It lengthens telomeres and shrinks tumor growth. It is antiaging as well as anti-inflammatory. It boosts the immune system, treats health conditions, seasonal allergies, heart problems, diabetes, and fight bacteria and infections like a chronic cough.
- *Gotu Kola*—a perennial plant that is used in traditional Chinese and Ayurvedic medicine and as culinary vegetable. It is a brain stimulant and memory booster. It decreases inflammation and decreases blood pressure in veins. It has been used for wound healing and skin disorders. It promotes the production of collagen. Gotu kola has been used to treat bacterial, viral, and parasitic infections. It is also used for psychiatric disorders. Do not take if you have liver problems or liver disease or are pregnant or plan on becoming pregnant.
- *Milk Thistle*—a flowering herb. It is being used for liver and gallbladder problems and decreases blood sugar levels as well as cholesterol.
- *Ashwaganda*—an evergreen shrub used in Ayurvedic medicine and is also called the Indian ginseng. It improves physical and mental health and treats memory loss, fever, diabetes, insomnia, and constipation. It also helps increase hemoglobin levels.

Anti-Cancer Superfoods

- Rubia
- Cordifolia
- Rhodiola
- Graviola
- Cherimoya
- Royal Jelly
- Holy Basil
- Moringa
- Bee Pollen
- Manuka Honey
- Chlorophyll
- Wheatgrass
- Patchouli Oil
- Cannabis Oil
- Wormwood
- Camu

Essential Oils—used to improve mental and emotional health. Some essential oils require to be used with carrier oils because of their high concentration levels. They can be used in various ways: a diffuser, a suppository, dropped under the tongue, topically, inhaled, rubbed under your feet, or rubbed on your skin, hair, nails, or spine. Add to your beauty and health regimen by making sprays, soaps, bed sprays, room fresheners, or lotions. Although some are ingested, I do not suggest ingesting essential oils because the high concentration in oils can put your body in shock and cause poisoning.

- *Lavender*—antibacterial/antifungal, reduces anxiety, promotes healthy sleep
- *Lemon*—antimicrobial, immunity stimulant, treats colds, bronchitis, and asthma
- *Peppermint*—helps digestion, relieves nausea, relieves muscle and joint pain
- *Rosemary*—improves circulation and concentration
- *Sandalwood*—promotes mental clarity, relieves itching, awakens sexual energy
- *Sage*—prevents bacterial infections, relieves inflammation of the stomach
- *Cedar Wood*—improves skin and hair health, cures rheumatoid arthritis
- *Juniper*—antiseptic, protects wounds, improves blood circulation
- *Bergamot*—lowers blood sugar and cholesterol levels, reduces fatty deposits
- *Frankincense*—helps relieve stress, reduces pain, and boosts immunity
- *Lemongrass*—relieves muscle pain, disinfects, wards off insects
- *Geranium*—treats acne, reduces inflammation, balances hormones
- *Myrrh*—reduces inflammation, alleviates pain, promotes wound healing
- *Tea Tree*—antibacterial/antifungal, treats acne, burns, and cold sores
- *Ylang-Ylang*—reduces stress, high blood pressure, headaches
- *Eucalyptus*—aids in decongestion, relieves muscular aches, natural repellent
- *Spruce*—restores depleted adrenal glands, treats asthma and colds
- *Chamomile*—anti-inflammatory, reduces anxiety and stress, helps you sleep
- *Cardamom Seed*—relieves asthma, spasm, and cramps
- *Tulsi Oil*—insect repellant, eliminates body odor, protects teeth and gums; should never be ingested

- *Oregano Oil P73*—can be ingested; however, it needs to be diluted in water or oil, such as olive oil. Oregano oil is a natural antibiotic that can be used to treat and heal numerous health ailments and health conditions. If you were to have one essential oil in your cabinet, this would be my pick. It is antiseptic, antibacterial, antifungal, antiparasitic, and anti-inflammatory. It is high in phenols, which have high antioxidant properties that protects from free radicals and toxins, defends against colds, flu, fights bacteria, relieves pain and headaches, has cancer fighting properties, helps aid in weight loss, lowers cholesterol levels, and protects against leaky gut. It can be applied topically to skin conditions and insect bites.

Food-Grade Oils / Organic, Extra Virgin, and Unrefined

- *Avocado Oil*—helps in nutrient absorption. Rich in vitamin B, omega 3, 6, and 9. A great cooking oil.
- *Coconut Oil*—should be virgin and cold pressed. It is great as a carrier oil for other essential oils. Naturally high in saturated fat, it has a high smoke point and can be used in baking and cooking. It can be used in your beauty routine; it removes makeup, moisturizes your hair and skin, and is great for oil pulling.
- *Argan Oil*—rich in vitamin A and E, it can be drizzled over meals. It is great as a carrier oil for other essential oils. It is also great for your beauty routine, as it replenishes dry skin, hair, and nails, and is great for oil pulling.
- *Olive Oil*—rich in monounsaturated fats and antioxidants. Protects against heart disease and stroke. Can be used as a cooking oil under low heat.

Kickbox Bad Habits to the Curb: Habit Don'ts

- *Smoking*—contains chemical that deteriorates your health in all body systems
- *Alcohol*—deteriorates brain functions and negatively impacts all body systems
- *Drug Abuse*—affects self-efficacy, self-awareness; destroys organs
- *Pharmaceutical Drugs*—abusing antibiotics can lead to inadequate recovery
- *Chewing Gum*—produces air pockets that upset your stomach; causes headaches
- *Snacking*—overeating causes weight gain and insulin resistance
- *Eating Too Fast*—causes digestive problems
- *Nail-Biting*—Increases bacteria and harbors infections
- *Phone / Radiation Exposure*—stop playing games; you're becoming a zombie
- *Foam/Plastic*—do not eat or drink from foam or plastic cups, plates, or bowls
- *Artificial Alkalized Water*—stop believing that a higher pH water is good for you. In reality, a higher pH that is artificially alkalized harbors bacteria.
- *Root Canal*—tooth becomes dead, which leads to anaerobic bacteria that can be toxic to your bloodstream.

Incorporate Good Habits: Habit Dos

- Sleep on Left Side—clears interstitial waste from the brain
- Eat/Sleep/Exercise—at the same times every day to get into a routine
- Shower before Bedtime—get into bed clean, without dirt and bacteria
- Wash Makeup Off—your pores need to breath, especially before bedtime
- Change Your Clothes and Underwear Daily—so you can be a clean human being!
- Read Labels—read food, body, cleaning labels, read all labels
- Wash Hands—before and after eating to reduce bacteria and viruses
- Have a Food Log—keeping track of your meals will help you make right decisions
- Chew Your Food—slowly and thoroughly. Eating too fast or swallowing your food can cause stomach issues and weight gain.
- Sun Exposure—increases vitamin D and guard against diseases
- Walk Barefoot—earthing increases antioxidant levels and reduces inflammation
- Use a Full Spectrum Infrared Sauna—relieves muscle pain, detoxifies, improves skin tone
- Perform a Kegel Squeeze—relieves urinary incontinence. Refer to online references and search engine.

CALISTHENICS

Calisthenics increases functional strength and flexibility, builds muscles, and improves endurance and mood by toning and activating glutes with your own body weight.

Basics

- Push-Ups—works out arms, back, and abs
- Jumping Jacks—elevates heart rate, tone muscle, relieves stress
- Pull-Ups—works back, arms, biceps, triceps; builds upper body strength

To Activate Glutes

- *Planks*—works back, arms, strengthens core, shoulders, and legs
- Squats—strengthens ligaments
- Box Jumps – Works calves, increases strength and muscle tone
- Burpees – Works chest, back, thighs, torso, shoulders, arms
- Deadlifts – Works back legs, hamstrings, spinal erectors
- Lunges – Works hips, hamstrings, and quads
- Hips thrust – Improve strength, speed, and power
- Clamshell – Helps with back pain and sciatica, improves hip strength
- Sprints – Works hamstrings, quads, hips, abs and calves

Rhythmic

- *Jump Rope*—engage in a three-minute rope jump to accelerate heart rate and tone body
- *Cardio*—at least four days per week, at least twenty minutes per day
- *Sex*—Have sex; it works all your body functions and improves heart health.
- *Weights*—1x per week
- *HIIT* (High Intensity Interval Training)—perform short period of intense anaerobic exercise. Reduces fats mass.

For reference and visual guide, refer to online sources:

- https://athleticmuscle.net/calisthenics-for-beginners
- https://www.shape.com/fitness/trends/what-is-calisthenics-workout-benefits
- https://www.progenexusa.com/blogs/science/total-calisthenics-workouts

HYGIENIC

Personal hygiene encourages confidence and dignity. Positive changes in human behavior lead to a more functional human being.

- *Face*—Wash your face and ears every morning. Wash makeup off every day.
- *Eyes*—Never share your face towel as it can carry trachoma and conjunctivitis that can harm your eyes.
- *Hair*—Wash at least twice a week to reduce skin infections such as *Tinea capitis*. Use a paraben-free and sulfate-free shampoo.
- *Body*—Engage in a whole body scrub 1x per week with a bristle brush. Do not use deodorant under your arms as it clogs your pores. If you feel you need to use deodorant, then use an organic deodorant without harsh chemicals and heavy metals. Use a shower filter to rid of chemicals that are present in tap water as they are hormone and immune disruptors. Do not use sunscreen that contains harsh chemicals and toxins; most sunscreens can cause skin cancer.
- *Oral*—Brush teeth twice daily with a fluoride-free toothpaste. Floss, oil pull, or mouth wash before bedtime.
- *Hands*—Maintain clean fingernails by clipping them and washing them daily. Use a paraben-free, sulfate-free, and fragrance-free hand soap.
- *Feet*—Maintain clean toenails and scrub feet daily.
- *Clothes*—Always wear undergarments and change garments daily.

LABELS

Identify labels of food, water, and beauty products.

Food Labels—When purchasing foods that are in jars, cartons, or packages, look for labels that include Certified NSF Gluten-Free, USDA Organic, Traceable, Non-GMO Verified, and BioChecked Non Glyphosate Certified.

Water Labels—When purchasing bottled water, look for labels that include USA Made, BPA/BPS Free, Pharmaceutical Free, Fluoride Free, MTBE Free, Chromium 6-Free, Arsenic Free, Chlorine Free, and Sodium Bicarbonate Free.

Tooth Paste Labels—When purchasing toothpaste, look for labels that include Fluoride Free. Usually the colored marker on the back of the tube will signify its chemical, artificial, or natural content. The Internet will tell you otherwise when it comes to toothpaste marker colors, however this is my experience:

- Red marker contains artificial and natural ingredients.
- Blue marker contains natural ingredients plus medications.
- Green marker contains natural ingredients.
- Black marker contains pure ingredients that are natural.

Shampoos and Conditioners—When purchasing shampoos and conditioners, avoid products with labels that contain parabens (methyl paraben, ethyl paraben, propyl paraben), which are linked to breast cancer. Avoid sulfates (sodium lauryl sulfate, sodium laureth sulfate), which damage the immune system. Avoid natural foaming and conditioning agents (cocamidoprophyl hydroxysultaine, cocamide DEA, behentrimonium chloride, isopropyl alcohol, silicones), all which are skin and eye irritants as well as strip the hair of natural oils.

Hand Soap / Laundry Detergent—When purchasing hand soap and laundry detergents, avoid purchasing products that contain synthetic colors (FD&C), fragrance (which is a secret formula), phthalates (plastics), and triclosan, all of which are endorphin disruptors.

Nail Polish—When purchasing nail polish, avoid those that contain dibutyl phthalate, toluene, formaldehyde, formaldehyde resin, and camphor, all of which cause reproductive harm and dizziness.

PERFUMES AND COLOGNES

How can smelling pleasant be disgusting?

Fragrances—Perfumes and colognes contain chemicals that are health hazards. Most people purchase perfumes and or colognes not considering the various harmful chemicals that are contained in each bottle. It would be wrong to completely blame the consumer because ingredients do not have to be disclosed, which is extremely frightening and alarming. Ever spray perfume or cologne and experience a mad headache or nausea? The fragrance industry has thousands of stock chemicals to choose from; imagine that.

Chemicals—Although you won't see the ingredients, which all can be labeled as fragrances (benzelbenzoate, diethyphtholate, tonacide), the common chemicals contained in perfumes and colognes cause headaches, nausea, wheezing, and asthma.

Natural Scents—Cardamom, cassia, cinnamon, lemongrass, lily, iris, lavender, violet, chamomile, yellow amber, cloves, myrrh, rose, cedar wood, sandalwood, and kyphi, are all natural scents derived from plants.

Natural Aphrodisiacs—Civet, musk, and ambergris are natural aphrodisiacs derived from animals. I personally would not use them, but I believe they are still a better option than fragrances.

FABRICS

The clothing you wear directly impacts your health.

Man-Made Fabrics—Contains toxic chemicals that damage your health by penetrating through the cell wall and causes changes to your cells. These toxic chemicals cause hormonal dysfunction, behavioral problems, and weight gain. The fabrics receive dyes, bleaching, softeners, and detergents. Look out for words like *wrinkle-free, anticling, antistatic, antishrink, waterproof, perspiration-proof, mildew-resistant, chlorine-resistant, stain-resistant, formaldehyde, brominated flame retardants,* and *per fluorinated chemicals*; all of which cause dizziness, nausea, headache, vomiting, muscle pain, insomnia, infertility, reduction in sperm count, respiratory diseases, rashes, itching, dermatitis, skin allergies, spine pain, Parkinson's disease, breast cancer, and lung cancer, among other cancers.

- *Rayon*—carbon disulphide, sulfuric acid, ammonia, acetone, and caustic soda
- *Acrylic*—highly flammable; made of polymethyl methacrylate
- *Polyester*—highly toxic; made from esters, dihydicalcohol, and terphalicacid
- *Spandex* – lycra, spandex, and elastane; made of polyurthane polymer
- *Acetate*—cellulosic fibers; made with acetatic acid and sulphuric acid
- *Nylon*—petroleum-based, caustic soda, sulfuric acid, formaldehyde, bleaching

Natural Fabrics

- *Cotton*—wear in all seasons, material adjusts to climate change
- *Silk*—keeps you cool in the summer and warm in the winter
- *Linen*—safe for all skin types, resistant to allergies; wear in warm weather
- *Wool*—dirt resistant, absorbs moisture; wear in colder weather
- *Leather*—absorbs water vapor, retains shape; wear in warm or cold conditions
- *Hemp*—similar to that of linen; derived from cannabis
- *Flax and Hemp*—can be used to replace synthetic fibers
- *Bamboo*—feels like silk and cotton, has a high antibacterial rate, has UV resistant qualities, pet resistant, suitable for hot and cool climate, makes you smell sweeter

LAB TESTED

Are you tired of guessing what works for you? Each and every single human being is unique in their own way, that being genetic makeup, blood type, and testosterone levels, all of which play a role in how our bodies react to certain foods and chemicals. Health conditions such as thyroid disorders may prevent us from losing weight, even when we are eating at our best.

Before changing your life, it is wise to ask your health provider for complete blood work, a thyroid test, and an allergy test to rule out discrepancies in your lifestyle. These tests will make your life much easier when you decide to make a lifelong change.

Smarter Cleaner Leaner

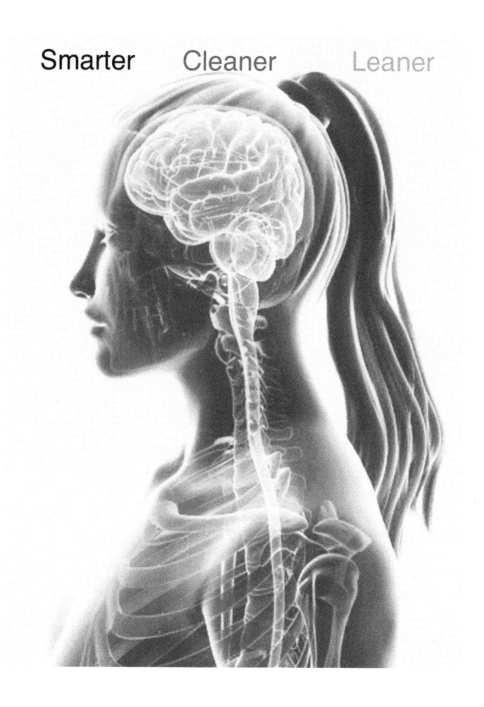

PRODUCT BRANDS

At times it is difficult to opt for healthier options because healthier foods require pre-paredness, thus greater amount of time and effort. If you are given the proper informa-tion to acquire products that are healthier alternatives, making a change will become much easier. Many times we are committed to making a change yet can be distracted by products at the market. In essence, I have compiled a list of healthier alternative products by brand name to be purchased by store or online. These products meet the requirements of the Healthy Lifestyle Guide and can be used to help you achieve your goals. In addition, continue to read product label composition and ingredients before making purchases due to the brand willingness to alter their recipes, ingredients or fabrics.

Water	Brand	Where to Purchase
Eternal	eternalwater.com	Whole Foods Market
Penta	pentawater.com	Whole Foods Market
Waikea	store.waiakeasprings.com	Plum Market

Juice	Brand	Where to purchase
Celery Root	Biotta	luckyvitamin.com
Beet Root	Biotta	luckyvitamin.com
Pure Tart Cherry	Lakewood Organic	luckyvitamin.com
Pure Prune	Lakewood Organic	luckyvitamin.com
Lemon Love	Suja	Plum Market

Milk	Brand	Where to purchase
Almond Malk	Malk	Whole Foods Market
Vanilla Almond Malk	Malk	Whole Foods Market
Grassmilk	Organic Valley	Whole Foods Market

Natural Sweetener	Brand	Where to purchase
Stevia	Wholesome!	Whole Foods Market
Luo Han Guo	Z Natural Foods	znaturalfoods.com
Maple Syrup	365	Whole Foods Market
Manuka Honey	Comvita	comvita.com
Monk Fruit	Lakanto	Whole Foods Market
Coconut Sugar	Laird Superfood	lairdsuperfood.com

Tea Brand	Where to purchase
Numiorganic Tea	Whole Foods Market
Choice Organic Tea	Whole Foods Market
Rish Tea	Whole Foods Market

Organic Herbs and Spices Brand	Where to purchase
Monterey Bay Spice Company	herbco.com
Frontier Co-op	Whole Foods Market

Bread Alternatives	Brand	Where to Purchase
Keto Thin Bread	Julian Bakery	julianbakery.com
Paleo Thin Bread	Julian Bakery	julianbakery.com

Pancake and Waffle Mix	Brand	Where to purchase
Keto	Birch Benders	Whole Foods Market
Paleo	Birch Benders	Whole Foods Market

Flours	Brand	Where to purchase
Coconut	Bob's Red Mill	Whole Foods Market
Almond	Bob's Red Mill	Whole Foods Market
Hemp	Bob's Red Mill	Whole Foods Market

Variety wraps	Brand	Where to purchase
Coconut wraps	NUCO	luckyvitamin.com

Condiments	Brand	Where to purchase
Mayo	Primal Kitchen	Whole Foods Market
Ketchup	Paleo Chef	Whole Foods Market
Maple Mustard	Paleo Chef	Whole Foods Market

Protein Bars	Brand	Where to purchase
Organic Fit	Garden of Life	Whole Foods Market

Spread Butter	Brand	Where to purchase
Peanut Butter	365	Whole Foods Market
Almond Butter	365	Whole Foods Market

Snacks Brand	Where to purchase
Rhythm Superfoods	Whole Foods Market
Peeled Snacks	Whole Foods Market
Cece's Veggie Co.	Whole Foods Market
Navitas Organics	Whole Foods Market

Alternative Cooking Utensils	Where to purchase
HexClad Cookware	hexclad.com
Zwilling	zwilling.com
Greenpan	greenpan.us

Essential Oils	Where to Purchase
Aura Cacia	Whole Foods Market
Garden of Life	gardenoflife.com

Toothpaste Brands	Where to Purchase
Jason	Whole Foods Market
Radius	Whole Foods Market
Schmidts	Whole Foods Market
Dr. Bronners	Vitamin Shoppe
Aesop	Aesop.com
David's	davids-usa.com

Makeup Brands	Where to Purchase
Bite Beauty	bitebeauty.com
Kjaer Weis	kjaerweis.com
Juice Beuty	juicebeauty.com
Lawless	lawlessbeauty.com
RMS Beauty	dermstore.com
W3LL People	follain.com
ZUZU LUXE	gabrielcosmeticsinc.com
Gabriel	gabrielcosmeticsinc.com

Shampoos and Conditioners	Where to Purchase
Rahua Shampoo	dermstore.com
Shea Moisture	sheamoisture.com
Christina Moss	christinamossnaturals.com
Intelligent Nutrients	intelligentnutrients.com
Juice Organics	juiceorganics.com
Nude	ahalife.com
Daniel Galvin Jr. Organic Head	danielgalvinjunior.com
Clean Kids Naturally	gabrielcosmeticsinc.com

Nail Polish	Where to Purchase
Ella+Mila	ellamila.com
Karma Organic	karmaorganicspa.com
Mineral Fusion	mineralfusion.com
Tenoverten	tenoverten.com

Skin Care Brands	Where to Purchase
Trilogy	trilogyproducts.com
Dr. Hauschka	dermstore.com
Juice Beauty	juicebeauty.com
The Ox Box	skincareox.com
Badger	iherb.com
Nurture My Body	nuturemybody.com
Kiss My Face Organics	kissmyface.com
Kari Gran	karigran.com

Deodorant Brands	Where to Purchase
Bubble and Bee	bubbleandbee.com
Soapwalla	soapwalla.com
Lume	lumedeodorant.com
Sedge & Bee	qhemetbiologics.com
Schmidts	shop.schmidts.com
Ursa Major	Ursamajorvt.com
Agent Nateur	agentnateur.com
Routine Natural Deodorant	routinecream.com
Dessert Essence	desertessence.com

Hand soap	Where to Purchase
Better Life	cleanhappens.com
Mrs. Meyers	mrsmeyers.com
Dr. Bronner's	drbronner.com

Cleaning Products	Where to Purchase
Better Life	cleanhappens.com
BioKleen	biokleenhome.com
Seventh Generation	seventhgeneration.com
Mrs. Meyers Clean Day	mrsmeyers.com
Branch Basics	branchbasics.com
Meliora Cleaning Products	meliorameansbetter.com
Dr. Bronners Pure Castile Soap	shop.drbronner.com
Earthworm	buyearthworm.com
Puracy	puracy.com
Truce	truceclean.com
Jaws	jawscleans.com

Natural Clothing Brands	Where to Purchase
Beaumont Organic	beaumontorganic.com
Bibico	bibico.co.uk
Bhumi	bhumi.com.au
Brooke There	brookethere.com
Groceries Apparel	grocereisapparel.com
Komodo	komodo.online
Know the origin	knowtheorigin.com
Kowtow	us.kowtowclothing.com
Kuichi	kuyichi.com
Kumikookoon	kumikookoon.com
Loomstate	loomstate.org
Noctu	noctu.co.uk
Pact	wearpact.com
Shift to Nature	shifttonature.com.au
Sorella Organics	sorellaorganics.com.au
Synergy	synergyclothing.com
Thought	wearethought.com

CONCLUSION

Today I am smarter, cleaner, and leaner at thirty-one than I was in high school, at age seventeen. Being the high school track and cross country MVP certainly led me to maintain a great physique running nearly five to eight miles daily. I was never a junk food junkie, and I was health conscious to a degree because I lacked the resources and knowledge to understand what I was consuming. Reminiscing back, there was all the "hype" to eat six times a day. Athletes alike were consuming high glycemic sports drinks and processed protein bars to ward off fatigue and build muscle. Two things we all had in common: number 1, we strived to be our best self, and number 2, we believed that exercise alone was the optimum solution to a better self.

After high school, I continued to exercise and eat what I thought was healthy. Among the so-called health foods I ate were hybridized wheat bread, low-fat milk, and tomatoes—all of which cause inflammation and fatigue. Getting married and having three kids for the next six years led me to gain a considerable amount of weight that became tedious to manage. I certainly did not feel my best, as my gut continued to protrude out with increased stress and irritability. Having memory fog and agonizing headaches was not a fun time to be me. I desperately tried every health trend and modern supplement, only to get bored of taking pills and give up on calorie counting altogether.

I knew this was no way to live. Exercise, pills, and calorie counting were not my strong suit. I needed a real solution—a solution that wasn't just going to make me leaner, but make me feel smarter, cleaner, and leaner. I started to research, and then I became the test subject of my experiments and the error or success of my trials. The most important fact I discovered was that *sugar* is the culprit behind most of my health issues, and that eliminating sugar from my regimen would get me on the path to be strong enough to make better health choices with a cleaner body and mind.

Be *smarter* by identifying false claims, understanding chemical compositions, reading labels, gathering reliable resources, and feeding your brain and not your stomach.

Be *cleaner* by recognizing bad habits, implementing health practices and protocols, maintaining personal hygiene, and seeking to prevent health ailments by using holistic healing modalities.

Be *leaner* by flavoring with organic herbs and spices, balancing macros and micros, using essential oils in your daily routine, consuming phytonutrients, and mastering calisthenics.

If you were given a test to complete with the answers on one sheet and an empty Scantron to fill in with the answers that were given to you, what do you think you would score? 99 percent–100 percent. Today you have the answers to achieve your health goals. Tomorrow starts today, and today is your tomorrow. I hope you have learned a great deal and **Stay Smart, Stay Clean, Stay Lean**.

CPSIA information can be obtained
at www.ICGtesting.com
Printed in the USA
LVHW071438120722
723335LV00020B/949

9 781643 459486